CHANGE YOUR LIFE

CHANGE YOUR LIFE

10 steps to get what you want

John Bird

Vermilion
LONDON

1 3 5 7 9 10 8 6 4 2

Published in 2008 by Vermilion, an imprint of Ebury Publishing

Ebury Publishing is a Random House Group company

The Random House Group Limited Reg. No. 954009

Addresses for companies within the Random House Group
can be found at www.rbooks.co.uk

A CIP catalogue record for this book is available from the British Library

The Random House Group Limited supports The Forest Stewardship
Council (FSC), the leading international forest certification organisation.
All our titles that are printed on Greenpeace approved FSC certified paper
carry the FSC logo. Our paper procurement policy can be found at
www.rbooks.co.uk/environment

Mixed Sources
Product group from well-managed
forests and other controlled sources
www.fsc.org Cert no. TT-COC-2139
© 1996 Forest Stewardship Council

Printed and bound in Great Britain by Clays Ltd, St Ives Plc

ISBN 9780091923549

Copies are available at special rates for bulk orders. Contact the
sales development team on 020 7840 8487 for more information.

To buy books by your favourite authors and register for offers,
visit www.rbooks.co.uk

This book is a work of non-fiction. The names of people have been
changed solely to protect the privacy of others.

CONTENTS

ACKNOWLEDGEMENTS

Thank you to Anita Roddick and the profundity of her legacy.

Thank you to *The Big Issue* teams who, over nearly two decades, have forged a wonderful path of change for the dispossessed.

Thank you to *The Big Issue* vendors who have used the paper to become a part of the solution, having once been a part of the problem.

Thank you to the inspiring poor of the world who drive the argument for justice forward.

And thank you Gordon Roddick, Nigel Kershaw, Ian MacArthur, Nic Careem, Eric Venus, Anne Garbarini, Tessa Bird, Paddy Bird, Diana Bird, Emily Bird, Parveen Bird, Sonny Bird, Ishpriya Bird, Anthony Epes, Peter Bird, Lucie Russell, Hannah and Charlie Russell Teare for giving me purpose when I most needed it.

INTRODUCTION

I was 15 when I first realised I could change my life. I was banged up in a young offenders' institution on the edge of London where I was locked in a cell for 23 hours of every day. I'd been dumped by my family and felt hated by all who knew me. I had no love, no hope, no comforts, only the prospect of being in prison for a few more years. I had never felt so low.

You might ask: how does a teenage boy end up in a prison cell? Well, it was like this. Born in a slummy part of Notting Hill in London, I was made homeless at a young age, along with four of my brothers. When I was seven we were put into a Catholic orphanage where we stayed for three years before the family was reunited in Fulham. But the problems did not end there. I became a very troubled boy – an arsonist, a truant, a shoplifter, a housebreaker. And all of this stemmed from those first 10 years when I thought I must be the worst kind of person for so many bad things to happen to me.

One day a prison officer came into my cell. 'Any requests, boy?' he said.

'No, sir,' I replied.

'What about a book?' he asked.

I gave him a look.

'Probably can't read a book, eh, boy?'

I didn't say anything.

He left, but returned later with a book. He threw it across the cell along with a pencil. 'Put a line under all the words you don't understand,' he said.

'I can read some, sir,' I replied defensively.

He said, 'Well, you've got some time on your hands to get better.'

Over the next few weeks the prison officer would look at the words I had underlined, one chapter at a time. He would then explain the words, and get me to write them down. He wasn't a teacher by profession, but a very kind human being, although he hid his kindness behind a gruff exterior. After a few weeks he said, 'You're not as daft as you look, are you?'

That prison officer was probably the most important person I ever met. He didn't patronise me or pretend things were better than they were. He just gave me support at a time when it looked as though I was heading for a life of crime and madness. I still struggle with reading. I still get blanks. My spelling is better, although it will never be effortless. But nobody can stop me from reading and writing, and continuously educating and informing myself.

Though I continued to make a pig's ear of my life, the seeds had been sown in that prison cell. I wasn't on the road to automatic failure. I could learn and I could change my life. And so can you.

A big part of my job today is giving talks and presentations about my life to inspire people – anyone from prisoners to property developers, via probation officers and government workers. Inspiring is a strange game. What you have to do is tell people what got you going, what helped you to change, what made you the person you are today. People normally expect you to have had one hell of a struggle, and they want a description of how you surmounted the most difficult of obstacles. So I seem to fit the bill, having come from a background of poverty, crime and homelessness before I became a helper to those in need.

But when I am sent the publicity material before my presentations I am always surprised at the words they use to describe my life, as if I have single-handedly wrestled a monster to the ground, or am a giant of hard work, hard living and hard character. It doesn't reflect the person I really am: someone who knows how to fight, but quite often loses; someone who got involved in creating *The Big Issue,* but was also accused of being incompetent and lacking in leadership, and of nearly destroying it.

I know it's kind of necessary to be built up as this great person who takes no prisoners and doesn't suffer fools gladly, so that people will want to come and listen to me. If I were presented as the very contradictory person that I am, then I might not be asked to give these talks. But the problem for me is that I do take prisoners and suffer fools, and sometimes I don't feel at all dynamic or worthwhile. And I want you to know this because otherwise the implication is that success and change for the good can only be achieved by great people who spend all their time being great. This is not true. The world is not full of icons, and you don't have to be a superhero to do something worthwhile.

So what I want to do in this book is tell the truth about my meandering road to success, with all the pitfalls and pit stops, in the hope that it will inspire you to feel that you too can change your life and make a contribution to the world. I want to share the experiences of my life, not so that you can say, 'Poor chap', or 'That's nothing, I had it twice as hard' – there are enough celebrity sob stories around. No, it is the lessons I have learned from my problems that are important. You can look at my life and realise, like me, that you should not be held back by your mistakes or limitations, but should instead turn them on their head and use them as the first steps on the road to success. More than anything, I want you to read this book and feel the blood rush to your head as you think: 'I can do it!'

One of the questions I am often asked is: when did I convert from being a pain in the rear to a useful person? And the answer is, gradually. By default, by mistake, by humiliation, by getting it wrong more times than right, by climbing out of the sticky stuff one step at a time, never straight and clean. And then, because I was not great, I soon realised that the greatness was in the work I was doing, as I moved from being part of the problem to becoming part of the solution. Very few things happen overnight, and, in my experience, nothing happens without effort and commitment, which is why this is not the kind of book that says you can be whatever you want. Or that you can solve all the problems in your life without even thinking about them. But it will, I hope, make you believe that change is possible and within your grasp; that we all have it within us to make things happen.

I remember giving a lecture at a college in the Midlands and afterwards being stopped by a woman who worked in the canteen. She said to me, 'You've made me think I shouldn't give up on my brother. He's got terrible problems with drugs. He's always doing something wrong against himself and us. But maybe there is something I can do for him. I'll try to get him some help.'

She walked on with a smile, then looked back and waved. I knew that whatever I had said she had been able to apply to her own problems. She had grasped the fact that I wasn't giving the lecture merely as some personality; I was there to be useful. Which is what I want this book to be: useful and relevant to you.

I often wish I had had a map for my life, to show me the way and point me in the right direction. When I moved to the city of Lille in northern France to write my autobiography I didn't take a map with me. I didn't know the beginning, middle or end of the city, so I got lost constantly. I would follow the road I thought was mine and end up in a dead end. Sometimes I would walk right past my house without realising it. For a few weeks Lille was unknown territory and hard to understand, until eventually I found my way around and got the hang of the place. It felt just like my life; I lost my way, then found it again. A good life map, if I had followed it, could have saved me many problems, heartaches and wasted opportunities. I hope this book will be a good map for you, and make changing your life a lot easier.

chapter one
MAKE A START WITH 3 PER CENT

The amount of times I am asked to explain how I achieved something as big as *The Big Issue* makes me realise that few people know how to cut something down to size. What they don't understand is that even the largest and grandest of projects is only made up of lots of little things. Breaking something big into small steps is the essence of what I call the 3 per cent rule. It is, I think, one of the most important pieces of advice in this book, which is why I'm starting with it, because it is what got me on the road to success, and it can help you to success, too. I did not move straight from poverty to purpose. I have made a long and hazardous journey of small steps – and the achievement of these small steps fills me with pride.

HOW THE 3 PER CENT RULE BEGAN

In the summer of 2007 I declared that I would be running as an independent candidate for the Mayor of London. I had many meetings, but one of the best meetings I had was in the posh offices of a large architectural business. I was the guest speaker at a lunch with loads of property developers who wanted to ask me questions about why I thought I should be Mayor and how I was going to achieve this huge goal. In order to answer them, I explained my 3 per cent rule by telling them this story:

When I was a boy I ran away from a young offenders' institution. I was caught, and when I got sent back my punishment was to dig over a big field with a spade and a pitchfork. The size of the area I had to dig was meant to overwhelm me. I knew they wanted not only to punish me but to defeat me and to see me fail, but I was determined not to let that happen. So I spent the first hour dividing the field into small squares. It made the task instantly more manageable and also meant I could measure my progress. Each time I did a square I felt I had achieved something, and this made it easier to keep going. By breaking down this enormous job into small parts, it was no longer daunting. I set myself a goal that

I could live up to. I started with 3 per cent, and each time I finished a square I added to that 3 per cent. I did not set myself up to fail and I showed the staff that I wasn't going to be defeated by their punishment. Even more importantly, I showed myself.

So I told some of the wealthiest people in London that this was how I would tackle the task of becoming Mayor of London: one small step at a time, 3 per cent followed by another 3 per cent until I reached 100 per cent. I then went through the 3 per cent steps I needed to take care of: getting supporters in every constituency to back my application to be put on the list of candidates; developing a press strategy; drafting a manifesto; encouraging people to vote on the day. Nothing was rocket science. It was just an accumulation of small things that, when added together, made up this grand event called the election.

In the end, I withdrew from the race to be Mayor of London. I realised that I would not be good at making excuses in the middle of the night for the failure of the planes, the trains or the drains. I am not an expert manager and I am no good at making apologies. Yes, I went for the wrong job, but not because I feared the vastness of the task. The 3 per cent rule rules OK!

3 PER CENT IN OUR LIVES

When you look around you, it is clear that the 3 per cent rule is already a part of our lives. For example, recently I have been looking at my very young children and marvelling at how much they have to learn. Anxiously I watch them as they learn to crawl – start, stop, stumble – all the little actions that go into a good crawl. And then suddenly they get it, and before you know it they are crawling with confidence. If you were ever to read a handbook on what a baby needs to achieve before she is able to even take her first step, you would break out in a worrying sweat. You would be overwhelmed by all the little 3 per cents that need to happen. But that is what we have all done, learned to walk and talk, and then gone on to develop even more skills.

So whatever project you want to tackle, however big or small, whether it is at work or at home, think in terms of 3 per cent. Set yourself up to succeed by making sure you are not trying to do too much, too quickly. It doesn't matter if you move slowly. As long as you are not standing completely still you are on your way. You'll see that there is no mystery to success. Anyone can do it – you can do it.

ONE STEP AT A TIME

When homeless people come to us at *The Big Issue* they are often broken wrecks. They have lost everything. How do you reconstruct a person who has been abused by life, and then abused themselves with alcohol, drugs and a rubbish diet? How do you put them back on the tracks of life? It would seem to require a giant step to change these people's lives.

But in fact, it doesn't. We don't ask these people for a giant step, because asking too much of anyone is just setting them (and you) up to fail. Instead we ask them to give us 3 per cent. Firstly, we ask them just to turn up on a regular basis. Once they've managed that, we ask them to sell *The Big Issue*. Then, gradually, we ask a little more. We ask 5 per cent. We might ask that they are well mannered, or that they don't drink on duty. Eventually we hope to increase it to 50 per cent in return for the 50 per cent we are giving them, so they give as much as they take. Similarly, we give them only what they need to stand on their own two feet.

All too often, big plans end in failure because too much is expected too quickly. This is why using the 3 per cent rule, reducing a big task into small, manageable steps, helps people to fulfil their dreams. The 3 per cent rule is the most natural way of achieving things. So don't be put off by the immensity of your ambition. Just get there one step at a time.

APPLYING THE 3 PER CENT RULE

The 3 per cent rule can be applied to anything you want to do in your life. I used it when I knew that I had to make some big changes to my lifestyle if I wanted to have an improving, healthier, more useful life. But I couldn't just say I was going to reform my life; I had to break it down into small steps. I knew I would have to give up the cigarettes, the drinking and the pursuit of the ultimate party – simple things, but not necessarily easy to do. So when I gave up smoking, I told myself that I wasn't going to smoke for a whole day. When I had done that, I increased the length of time to a week. In seven days I was there, and then another week and another week until I hadn't smoked for a whole month. So whether it's giving up smoking, or drinking or going on a diet – if you break it down into small steps, you will find your goal much easier to achieve.

SMALL STEPS, GIANT ACHIEVEMENT

Giant steps are only made by giants. But an accumulation of small steps can look like a giant achievement in the end, even if it isn't planned.

A friend of mine created an important audio business, which wins all sorts of prizes. He employs lots of young people to run his stores who have often had limited prospects, but he gives them the chance, and very few of them let him down.

I asked him how he single-handedly started up his highly successful business. He tells me it was at school when he started to buy second-hand audio equipment. He would get it repaired, and then sell it through a magazine. He started off making pennies, then pounds. Out of this he opened his first shop. And out of that grew the chain that bears his name.

In the shop he remembers the 3 per cent rule all the time, the little things he has to do to keep the staff working and feeling empowered.

Remember, enjoy and celebrate your gains no matter how small. You went walking for 20 minutes? Great. Don't worry that your best mate went running for an hour. It is *your* goal that matters – and *your* life.

DON'T BE SCARED

Applying the 3 per cent rule to your life helps to take the fear out of what you want to do. When you reduce everything to little steps, big things stop being so frightening. That's what I did when I divided the field in the young offenders' institution all those years ago: I was taking the fear and the sense of despair out of the job. Later in my life, I had to do something similar a few weeks before the launch of *The Big Issue* in the US.

The launch was a big event. We had done everything we could, but the team of writers, designers and distributors was nervous. We all sat down, and I listened to them talk about the problems of the launch. Each problem was presented as being virtually insoluble.

Even though we had put a progress chart on the wall so that people could see what stages we needed to complete before we went on to the next, I realised that they were frightened we had bitten off more than we could chew. It was crunch time. To stop the fear and convince my team they could do this launch, I needed to break things down once more. I had to show that we just needed to take small steps to achieve our goal, and that we would only succeed if the team stopped being so afraid.

A few weeks later we had the best launch ever. It was organised, structured and almost perfect, a big event with great coverage on TV, radio, newspapers and magazines.

I have never done anything in this world that required the knowledge of rocket science. As a child I learned to walk, then to talk and then to use these two skills to create others. I did not change my life by giant steps, from poverty to purpose. I have made a long and hazardous journey of small steps – and I am proud of my achievement because I believe the 3 per cent rule is one of the best ways of helping people to help themselves.

So next time you want to make something happen in your life try this: set a goal you can achieve. What I mean is that you need a goal that doesn't rely on luck, or chance, or anybody else coming through for you. It has to be real, and not pie-in-the-sky stuff. That doesn't mean it has to be small. Just make sure it's within your grasp.

If you are put off by big projects, or feel that you would love to achieve something big but don't know how to get there, or want to make a change in your life but feel overwhelmed by the task ahead, then try the 3 per cent rule. I truly believe that it is one of the best ways of helping people to help themselves. Try it. In fact, you are probably already doing it in your everyday life. Just make it a conscious thought when you plan your goal. Think big, but get there small.

- Identify the little things you need to do, and divide the task up into these small, simple steps.

- Be realistic about your ability to deliver each step. Don't try to make the steps bigger than you can manage. You will only be setting yourself up to fail.

- Be prepared to put in the time, and be patient. Time as well as effort will be needed to achieve your goal.

- Enjoy each step that you take, however small, and congratulate yourself every time you achieve something. Be joyful about it. Enjoy the change that you are bringing into your life.

chapter two
BE YOUR OWN LEADER

Before you start to make changes in your life ask yourself these questions:

- Are you controlling your own life and making your own decisions?

- Or are you following someone else's lead, allowing someone else to make the decisions in your life or trying to fulfil other people's expectations?

- Are you taking responsibility for your own life?

It doesn't matter whose expectations you're trying to live up to, however well-meaning the people – your mother, your brother, your partner or lover. If you want to make the most of your life and realise the potential of your skills and learning, you have to decide to be your own leader. Don't be afraid of taking responsibility for your life.

BELIEVE IN YOURSELF

To do this you need to believe that you can be your own leader. You need to believe in yourself and the fact that you can change your life. I know how difficult this can be because for most of my childhood and young adult life I didn't believe in myself or my ability to do anything other than follow the life I'd been born into. I would think: if only I'd been born to a mum and dad who filled the house with classical books and pianos and had a holiday home in the Alps. But I was brought up in the slummy surroundings of the Portobello Road, one of six children, and we were living in a state of permanent crisis. My parents were unable to look after their money – Mum thought cigarettes were more necessary than paying the rent – and their children, which was why I was sent to an orphanage at the age of seven. So I was marked out for a life of trouble. I didn't believe there was any other way to be.

It was even worse when I went to school. When you're wearing the dirtiest and roughest clothes because you can't afford the school uniform, when you can't pay for school dinners, something happens: you feel as though you've gone down a few notches in other people's eyes and in your own. I believed the teachers and staff were my enemy right from the start. So the only boys in school I had time for were boys who were in trouble, like me. We were living the life we thought was expected of us. We all believed we were destined for prison. And that's where many of us ended up, including me. And of course, once you start to believe you're marked out for trouble, you get a reputation for bad behaviour, which makes it harder to think differently about yourself.

At school I was once accused of something I hadn't done by my teacher. He was always sending me to the head for a caning, and told me I was the one person he wished wasn't in his class. At the beginning of every week he would collect the dinner money. One Monday, after doing all his adding up, he was a pound short. The teacher was beside himself. Someone, he reasoned, had stolen the pound. He asked the class who was responsible; we all denied it. Then he asked us who we *thought* had done the stealing.

I already had a bad reputation as the dirty, scruffy git who was always at court, so it was a done deal. The teacher took me out into the corridor and asked me to empty my pockets. I refused, so he said that I would have to go to the headmaster.

The next day came and the teacher took me into the corridor again and told me that the pound had been found. He had added up the dinner money wrongly. Even then I knew that this would not be the last time, I would always be blamed when something went wrong.

Sports day was another occasion when the 'bad boys' were shown up. For one reason or another none of us had any kit. With me it was because my family was poor and my parents didn't want to waste what money they did have on sport's kit. I don't know about the other boys, but whatever the reason it meant we never got the chance to run. But one sports day I was lent some kit so I could participate in the eliminations. The sports teacher was surprised to see me lining up for the one hundred yards – and even more surprised when I won two heats and then came second in the third heat. His response was to put the boy who came third in my place. So I didn't get to run on the big track in front of the school, its teachers and its governors. He didn't give a reason but even though I was only twelve at the time I knew why he was ruling me out. I was a trouble-maker on the fast track to the inside. I was going nowhere worth following.

These were the expectations other people had of me and I had of myself. I didn't believe I could do anything that would change the direction of my life. Crime was the outcome. Within months of leaving school I was sentenced to a young offenders' institute for three years for receiving money under false pretences. I'd cashed a shop savings book that a friend had stolen from his granny's house. At the time I had no sense of doing anything wrong or, if I did, I didn't care. But now, because I have been involved in crime, I am more determined to help prevent other people falling into it.

MAKE YOUR OWN DECISIONS

At first, I was determined to stay out of trouble in the reformatory. If I played my cards right, I thought, I might get out in two years. So I got my head down for a while. Then I started to get into trouble. So, with another boy, I conspired to run away.

The day we had planned to run away I had been put up a grade, from novice to lower. I was astonished and delighted – obviously I hadn't been as bad as I thought. But the other boy had a contract with me, or so he thought. He was having a worse time than me, and was desperate to get out and stay out. It was a toss-up whether I stayed or went.

I went. We got to London, stole a car and a few hours later smashed it up, driving at about 100 miles per hour. Neither of us was hurt. In court I was remanded to a boys' prison where I waited until they caught the other boy. Months later we were reunited in court. The head of the young offenders' institution spoke up for me, and said he felt I had been misled. I said that was not true, that running away was my decision.

My decision? What crap. I didn't know or believe I was capable of making real decisions; at least, not ones that could change my future. I was just living the life expected of me, rather than leading one of my own choice. We often behave badly because we think that is what is expected of us. But doing what is expected of you is a sure sign that you are not leading, or taking a lead in your own life. Making your own decisions means you can start to take control of your life.

THINK FOR YOURSELF

To be able to make your own decisions, you need to know your own mind and think for yourself. It isn't easy being an original thinker. We live in a world where we have information, and other people's opinions and prejudices, coming at us from every angle, and it can seem much easier and less tiring just to accept them. But if you go through life without questioning what you are being told and without thinking for yourself, you can't lead your own life. Taking on other people's ideas and not having your own will hold you back, and stop you from developing and progressing as far as you could in life.

Recently I met a man with a lot of experience in running a business and managing people. I was thinking about employing him because I wanted to expand *The Big Issue* into new businesses, so I sat down with him and told him about all the various projects I was involved in. I explained I was spreading myself too thin and needed help, and asked him what he felt he could do. He said, 'I'll do whatever you want me to do.'

I was astonished. I had thought of hiring this man to be his own person, to think for himself, to have original ideas and make his own decisions. I wanted him to use the leadership skills I knew he had. How could he be a leader if he didn't think for himself and just followed me?

Work is often about routines. But even routines need to be changed sometimes. If you want to progress from shelf-stocking in the supermarket, for example, you need to take the lead in your job and question how the routine is working. Is it capable of improvement? Is there another system that will do the job more efficiently?

Some companies are smart, and tap into the knowledge and brains of their staff by rewarding ideas they might have for improving work and saving money. One of the best examples of this must be the Bryant & May match company. A suggestion from a member of staff saved the company hundreds and thousands of pounds. It was simple: they only needed to have sandpaper on one side of the matchbox, not both sides.

BE YOURSELF

When I was a teenager in the early 1960s I thought that being yourself meant being as different as possible from your parents and that a lot of it was to do with how you expressed yourself on the outside. In fact, I wasn't quite sure who I was, but I knew who I wasn't – I wasn't like my father: a hard worker. There was no way I was going to be found on a building site at 7 a.m.

I was going to be something special, something different. So, at the age of 15, I decided to become a beatnik. Beatniks were like an earlier version of hippies, though not as loving and cuddly. They were often beggars, scroungers and sometimes thieves. And they tended to write very bad poetry. So I did the same. I wore the uniform – dark clothes, torn Levis, long, dirty hair – and I carried a notebook in which I wrote what I believed was poetry.

It wasn't until quite a few years later that I discovered being yourself is not really about the clothes you wear on the outside; it's about what you think on the inside. To be yourself means thinking for yourself and owning the ideas you hold.

Examine your thoughts before they become a part of your thinking. When I started *The Big Issue* I had to demonstrate that I had my own ideas, and that I wasn't just following the rest of the homeless charity world. I had to think for myself. It was clear that homelessness was a huge problem and that the current thinking wasn't working. Someone had to come up with something different.

I did. I came up with solutions for homeless people so that they could get some discipline and order into their lives. I thought of a way to give homeless people the chance to make their own money and have the same opportunities that we have when we go to work. My ideas weren't particularly startling or complex. But the thoughts and the actions that came from them were mine. I owned them; they had filtered through my thinking.

I'm not saying that your opinions have to be different from everyone else. You don't have to struggle to be original. Just try to be thorough and thoughtful. You may well hold the same opinions as the herd. The difference is that if you have taken hold of your ideas you have thought them through. They are yours, even if they are shared by a hundred million people. You have worked on them and you can claim ownership of them. Keep thinking and keep owning.

DON'T WAIT FOR SOMEONE ELSE TO TAKE THE LEAD

If you wait for someone else to take the lead, nothing may ever happen. There are too many people who think it's always up to someone else. I have always chosen to take the lead when I have had the chance, especially when others don't or can't.

I remember once being taken on a kind of adventure holiday in the Peak District with the young offenders' institution when I was a teenager. It was supposed to be character-building, and we were given a tough instructor who drove us hard and made us walk for miles and climb lots of hills. On the last-but-one day we were coming down a hill when a storm blew up. Hailstones as big as golf balls began to fall. We were all cowering behind a wall but the instructor stood up and told us that we had to get down the hill as soon as possible. He could see we were getting drenched and losing both our body warmth and our spirit.

The troop wouldn't move. We stayed behind the wall. It was harder to go down the hill than stay where we were. Suddenly something within me made me stand up, and I shouted, 'Down the hill, boys, down the hill!' I started to sing and shout and rally them. They all got up and started to sing and shout, too, ignoring the bad weather that engulfed us. Half an hour later, soaking, tired and hungry, we were in the safety of the van on the valley floor.

I had taken the lead. If I'd waited for somebody else to do it we might still be up on that hill.

DON'T BLAME OTHER PEOPLE

I am always meeting people who make excuses for the mess their lives are in, and say to me, 'He made me do such and such', or 'I did such and such because of her'. Even members of my own family have told me they were doing things for me. But there isn't an evil fat controller hidden in a cave somewhere, controlling your life, making you do things you don't want to do. You can change your life but it's up to you to do it. You alone are responsible for your life, so make sure it's good.

- Believe in yourself and the fact that you can make a difference.

- Make sure you don't mindlessly follow the person in front.

- Think about what you're doing first.

- Take responsibility for your actions.

- Don't be the one who says, 'I was only following orders.'

- Remember: you only have one life – as the saying goes, it is not a dress rehearsal.

- Get a life – and make sure it's your own.

chapter three
LEARN FROM OTHERS

You may be the brightest kid on the block, and capable of being your own leader, but it's important to remember that even the greatest leaders still have to learn from others. In fact, the greatest leaders on earth are the ones who know how to listen and follow the example of good leaders before them. How else can you know your own mind if you have not learned from the minds of others?

So, whatever it is you want to do or achieve in life, whether it's acquiring a new skill or developing a talent you already have, or changing something in your life, you will be most successful if you are prepared to listen to other people's experiences in that area. For me, being prepared to do this has sometimes even saved my life. It wasn't always easy to learn from other people, especially when I was a lot younger and thought I knew it all. Then it was very hard to accept that someone might be worth listening to, that they might know more about a particular subject than me. But if you can overcome your pride and be humble enough to learn from someone else's know-how, you will find that you can achieve your goals much more quickly.

APPRENTICESHIP

Everyone needs role models: people we can learn from, people to look up to and respect, who set an example of how life can be lived. In the old days we used to have apprenticeships. You would learn your trade by working as an apprentice. You didn't earn much money but what you gained was knowledge and skill, so that one day you'd be ready to do the job yourself. It was automatic to listen to those with experience and to learn from them. Although formal apprenticeships may not be common today, it is no less important now than it was then to learn what you can about life from those with experience. So listen to other people, see what they have to say, and gain knowledge both about yourself and the world.

One of the first times I properly understood the importance of listening to other people was when I was just 15 and homeless. I'd been on the run for a while after jumping bail, moving from city to city, and finally ended up back in London where I'd been sleeping rough in the west and east of the city. When I moved into the West End and started begging there, I noticed a man watching me. After a while he came up to me and introduced himself as James.

'I'll take you for the best value breakfast in the West End,' he said.

I'm not sure what made me go with him. Curiosity, perhaps, although I had heard of someone named James and thought he might be worth listening to.

As we walked along the Strand, James said, 'I can tell you're new because you're open begging. No one open begs near Cannon Row. If the police get hold of you, you'll get the kicking of your life before they put you before a court. And, though they're not supposed to, they will fingerprint you.'

I was only 15 but I had had my dabs done already, which meant if I was picked up now and fingerprinted they would know I was on the run for jumping bail and should be taken to court to face up to the charge of receiving money under false pretences. James walked quickly, urgently, despite a limp. I kept up with him but I had no energy; after sleeping rough for a few months I was constantly tired.

Eventually we came to a small, half-empty café. I bought my own breakfast, enjoying the knowledge that I was spending money I had made from my own begging. I was used to begging – I even used to beg money for my mother's cigarettes. I didn't find it difficult and rejection didn't bother me. Did I really need to listen to some old-timer who was going to tell me how to survive on the streets of the West End?

'I can give you a lot of information,' James began. 'I can help you while you're begging in my manor, but I can't think for you.'

I sat back. I didn't want to be told what to do, even if he was king of the beggars. I had been getting buses up to the West End since I was 10 and had left the orphanage. I knew the roads and some of the clubs; James spoke like he didn't even come from London.

'No open begging,' he continued. 'No sleeping on park benches, day or night, except in St James's Park, and then only in the bushes. No robbing, no handbag-snatching. This is a good part of London to work the streets, but you've got to do it quietly, and without being noticed. There are people who will want to use you: as a boy for men, as a shoplifter, as a beggar while they take the lion's share. There are all sorts of ways of using a boy your age, so you need to find a way of not getting noticed and of avoiding certain places where they'll prey on you. Understand?'

I said yes, but I meant no. He was boring me. I could look after myself. I was tougher than I looked.

Then a young-looking bloke came in. His bulging arms sported many tattoos. He wandered up to us, looked at me as though I was a good meal – or a good meal ticket – and said to James, 'So who's the pretty boy, eh?'

James grabbed the bloke and pulled him down to his face. 'He's a cousin of mine.'

'Sure, Jimmy.' The bloke spluttered his apology, like something out of a bad film.

'Micky,' James said after the bloke left the café, 'is a pimp. He pimps little boys and little girls. Or should I say, he works for a pimp; he just gets the goods. You are the goods. I'm not trying to frighten you, but I wouldn't stay in the West End. You're fresh meat to the pimps. You're just a kid, a boy who can't go home because he's done something wrong. So go home, face the music, or end up being a boy on the game.'

I hadn't wanted to listen to James; I was young and arrogant enough to think I didn't need anyone else's advice. But for some reason I did listen to him, and this saved me from rape, abuse, drugs and all the other things that can fall upon a 15-year-old who wanders away from home. I learned, very quickly, how important it is to remember you don't know it all. I left the West End and went back to the streets I knew, keeping in the background during the day, and only coming out at night. I begged quietly. But one night the inevitable happened and I didn't need to worry about pimps any more. I was caught, taken to the police station and put before a court.

HUMILITY

I have already talked about the importance of being your own leader in life. Some people think being a leader means doing what you think is right and ignoring everyone else. It doesn't. The best leaders are the ones who know that they are not always right and learn from other people. It is not always easy accepting that you need to learn from someone else, that you can always improve, but there are many times in life when you have to swallow your pride and act with humility. This means accepting that you don't know everything and that you always have something to learn, that you can always improve. It is, I think, one of the most difficult lessons to learn, but one of the most important. All the people I most admire, men and women who have achieved great things, are still humble and recognise their limitations and that they have more to learn.

Humility was certainly a quality I needed when I was starting up *The Big Issue*. Although we had the financial backing and a name, we needed credibility and the support of those working within the homeless sector. If one of the many organisations working with the homeless would give us their blessing, this would help us talk to the police so that we could talk to the homeless. Without their endorsement, launching *The Big Issue* would be very hard, if not impossible.

For this reason I found myself standing in Trafalgar Square before a bearded man, probably a few years younger than me, who said: 'You know nothing about the lives of the homeless. You're a million miles from their experiences.' It was clear this man, someone who worked for an organisation to help the homeless, didn't like me or the fact that I was going to start a street paper without being one of the homeless charities. His assessment was based on a meeting we had had with a group of homeless people a few hours earlier. He had been very patient and careful with them, and didn't like it when I said I felt he had been too soft with them. He was prepared to talk to me because the organisation he represented didn't want to drive away the well-known philanthropist Gordon Roddick (co-founder of The Body Shop with his wife Anita) who was backing *The Big Issue* and might be persuaded to help them – but it was obvious he didn't trust me. His view was the same as most people who worked in the sector at that time: that the last thing the homeless needed or wanted was a legitimate way of making money. They were people with deep, deep problems who needed psychological and physical help; to be given their own place of safety and lots of attention; to be helped into doing something more useful than selling a street paper on the streets of London to an (at times) angry, dismissive public. Anyway, he didn't believe we could get either the homeless to sell or the public to buy.

I didn't like being told that I knew nothing. But it was 30 years since I had been homeless myself, long before organisations to help the young homeless ever existed. Listening to the bearded man made me realise that I needed to understand the contemporary problem of homelessness as well as what was being done to solve that problem. I had to be prepared to swallow my pride, to listen to people telling me what to do, even if I didn't necessarily respect them. And I realised he was right when he told me that I had to go and talk to the homeless. I needed to find out what they were capable of. Could they write for the publication? Could they help with the design? Would they sell the paper when it came out? If *The Big Issue* was ever going to be more than just an idea I had to get closer to the homeless. Only then would I know whether or not our street paper would be any use.

Listening to the bearded man, someone who had a lot of experience in working to help the homeless, helped me much more than I at first realised. I learned what was being done for the homeless, I listened and served my apprenticeship, and I left knowing that I had to do something very different. If I had not learned from him I would never have known what to do.

IMPROVE

Once you have listened to and learned from other people, then you can begin to develop your own style and improve on what you have learned. I started *The Big Issue* in opposition to all that was being done for homeless people at that time. I did my research, my apprenticeship, then found another way, which was to give homeless people an alternative to begging; to provide an income rather than a dependency on handouts. I had to improve on the existing homeless model, which was not giving people the way out of homelessness. In fact, the numbers of homeless were then rising.

If you want to do something well, and better than it has been done already, you have to understand and really grasp the essential nature of what you are trying to improve.

- Be humble enough to listen to the opinions of others, and withhold judgement until you know what you're talking about.

- Resist the temptation to be original for the sake of it.

- Learn the basics. You do have to walk before you can run.

- Be patient and serve your time. Learn to endure the conflict between what you wish to do and what you have to do.

chapter four
LEARN FROM YOURSELF

A few years ago I appeared on a TV show. I had not prepared for it and thought I could get by just shooting from the hip. But the interviewer could see I wasn't being clear – I hadn't been thinking about what I was saying – and threw in some sharp questions about *The Big Issue*. It felt like an attack.

As I left the studio and walked down the road, feeling bruised, I was cross with myself. Why had I left it to someone else to ask the hard questions? Why hadn't I been asking them of myself? Self-interrogation was something I used to do, but I'd gradually forgotten the importance of it.

Now I can say that I have never found a better method of identifying the changes I need to make in my life than by looking at myself with detachment, as an interviewer. It may sound strange, but I suspect you'll be amazed by what you discover about yourself.

HOW TO INTERROGATE YOURSELF

Of course, you have to ask the right questions – and the simpler the better. Rather than daydream about being rich and famous, your first question could be: 'What's stopping me from changing my life or getting to where I want to be?' A bloke I know always tells me that his lack of skills is preventing him from getting a better life. So then I ask, 'What's stopping you getting the skills?' This might lead to a long list of reasons, such as lack of money, time or dedication. In the end you may come to the conclusion that you need outside help and can't do it all yourself. But start by asking this simple question, then ask yourself what you can do to get rid of the obstacles that are in your way.

You won't learn anything about yourself unless you're prepared to be tough. So pretend you're being inter-viewed by Jeremy Paxman rather than a journalist from *Hello!* magazine, and demand the truth from yourself. Find a comfortable place, but make sure the questions are uncomfortable.

One of the best things about conducting your own interview is that you can do it anywhere and at anytime, although you need to allow yourself time to think through the questions and your answers. I find that walking clears my mind and helps me clarify my thoughts. I can walk for miles without realising how far I've gone because I'm so focused on my thoughts and internal interview. After my disastrous television interview I walked all over London asking myself dozens of questions about what I was doing with my life, and trying to find some kind of truth. I made a start, but there were too many questions to answer all in one go. I needed to give myself a bit of a break before doing it again, but I knew I would because I'd woken up to the fact that I had to learn from myself.

A few months later I decided to walk to Smithfield market and have an early-morning breakfast in my favourite café. (For some reason I need to be away from my usual environment for the really big questions.) Although I hadn't planned the questions I was going to ask myself beforehand, I knew in my head what questions I wanted answers to. I began by asking myself where I was going with my life. What was the purpose of the struggle that had led me from poverty to comfort, from obscurity to reputation? Was it to produce a street paper that would help the homeless to help themselves? And then leave it to others? I had brought in new people to deal with the financial problems and we were getting stronger. I was more hands-off. But what was I going to do with the extra time?

ANSWER TRUTHFULLY

Halfway through my egg, bacon and beans on toast I stopped. All my cross-questioning was fine in the abstract. But the answers to my questions were just as important – if not more so – and they were only useful if I was completely honest about myself. Honesty doesn't come easily; the tendency to lie to yourself is strong. But if I was going to make any changes to my life, I had to learn the truth about myself so that I could change what I didn't like.

And there was quite a lot I didn't like about my life at that time. My self-interview revealed a life of absolute confusion. I was separated, living on my own, a born-again bachelor in my mid-fifties heading towards eternity with only a reputation to show for it. I was getting all the exercise in the world but I was eating badly, and smoking and drinking too much. I was taking the edge off my life. I was meeting dozens of people a week, including some charming women, but could not remember an awful lot about them. And I was drinking with people who, like me, were living on former glories. I was drifting in all ways and in all directions.

I began to think of an incident at a reformatory when I was 17. I had behaved badly and kicked another boy into a foul-smelling pond. When it was time for me to appear before the committee for an assessment of my release date the governor asked me the key question: 'Do you believe you should leave, Bird?' Thinking objectively about my situation and my behaviour, I replied, 'No, sir, I don't. But I would like to.' It was an honest and thoughtful answer. The committee were so delighted with this rare glimpse of self-awareness and honesty that they decided to allow me to leave as soon as I had a job to go to, believing that this honesty was an indication of maturity.

DO SOMETHING ABOUT THE ANSWERS

It was all well and good asking myself tough questions, answering them honestly and discovering truths about myself, but the next step was to do something about what I'd learned. My interrogation had to have a practical outcome. Action was needed.

I decided to start by concentrating on myself. I vowed to quit the drinking, the smoking and the empty social-ising. I became determined to find a way of using my skills and abilities to put some life back into what I was doing with homeless people.

That day, having interrogated myself about my life, asked the right questions and faced up to the answers, I started to change and improve my life. So now I do not smoke, rarely drink, and have given up chasing the social scene. The strength to do this came from facing up to the naked truth about myself.

KEEP MENTALLY ACTIVE

We are only beginning to understand the importance of brain training. The popularity of puzzles such as Sudoku and computer games for the brain demonstrates that there is a growing awareness of the need to keep mentally as well as physically active.

The more you use your brain the healthier and fitter it becomes, so making yourself answer your own questions is like giving your mind a good workout. You will begin to take challenges in your stride and overcome problems more easily. You will sharpen your concentration and improve your memory. How many times do you watch a film, read a book, or attend a meeting, and forget it all a few days later? Taking the time to discover your thoughts or opinions on films/books/meetings will make the subject stick, and is also a good way of learning more about yourself. So don't forget to ask yourself the questions, and make yourself strong by learning from your answers. There is no point in asking yourself the questions, getting to the answers and then ignoring what they tell you.

Learn what you need to do and then get on with it. Take action on the answers and embrace the actions. But do it by easy steps. Try the easy things first and enjoy doing some of the simple things you have learnt from your answers.

- Try planning the questions. You might even choose to write them down, because it is easy to allow your mind to drift away from the important point.

- Keep your questions focused so that you can do something with the knowledge you gain from them.

- Ask yourself tough questions. These are the most important ones. Remember: you are asking these questions to gain self-knowledge, which will help you to make the changes you need in your life.

- Be honest. If you are honest to yourself about yourself, then you can be honest with other people and so gain their trust and respect.

- Be prepared to do something about the answers. Make sure there is a practical outcome. Don't kid yourself that knowing and understanding your situation is enough.

- Have fun learning about yourself. Enjoy the process of building self-knowledge and creating new ways of solving problems yourself.

- Learn what you need to do and then get on with it. But apply the 3 per cent rule: take small steps. Try the easy things first and enjoy doing them.

chapter five
PLAN YOUR GOALS

We all need goals to give our lives direction. Without something to aim for, and a plan to get there, life becomes something you drift through without accomplishing anything. I should know: I have lived much of my life without knowing where I was going, just relying on chance to get me through. It has only been relatively late in my life that I can see how much time and energy I wasted not having achievable goals (big or small) with an effective plan, and how important it is not to let life just happen. So whatever your goal is in life, whether it's big or small, make sure you have a plan for getting there.

Everything we do involves a plan. We have to plan to get to work, or where to meet someone for lunch. If you decide to make an omelette, then maybe the first thing you need to do is wash up the frying pan. But the big things also need a plan. And we have to make that plan as simple as possible.

A woman who now works with me planned her progression from making sandwiches into becoming an accountant. She prepared every stage, even the time she would need to read books and travel to her weekly classes. Each part of the plan was simple, but she took each necessary step. And in the end she got there.

SET YOURSELF AN ACHIEVABLE GOAL

Before you make a plan, make sure you have a goal that is realistic; the big mistake of most of my life has been having goals I couldn't achieve. And if you set your goal too high, you are in danger of never reaching it.

At the age of 16, when I was banged up in the young offenders' institution, I became interested in art. After a few months of learning more about art, I decided that I wanted to be a painter. And if that had been my goal, perhaps I would have succeeded. But my goal was to become the best artist there ever was. My plan was simple but hugely ambitious: I would paint and draw all the hours that I could in that institute, and when I was out and free again I would carry on until I got a place in a top art school and became the world's best painter. I would paint from first thing in the morning until last light.

My plan worked initially: when others in the institute were enjoying their rest time I would try to draw a pot of geraniums, or anything else around me. Later, when I left and got a job, I attended evening classes in drawing every night of the week and then, waking exhausted on a Saturday morning, would go off to the parks to paint and draw in the open air.

My hard work paid off. I got into a top art school. I became good, very good. I was adored by my teachers and taken seriously. I was full of hope and potential.

But I couldn't keep it up. I couldn't keep on doing nothing but drawing all day. I had set my goal too high and made my plan too difficult to achieve. Of course, what happened was that the minute a young girl came my way, and I was distracted, my plan instantly fell apart. Instead of drawing in the studio, I spent time with this girl. My goal was too ambitious and my plan too hard to achieve. It was 'all or nothing' and, as I couldn't do it all, I ended up with nothing.

The greatest regret of my life is that I never became that painter, never spent my days with the smell of paint and canvas, and that I abandoned my goal. The sad thing was that my plan was working. In fact, I achieved a lot, but because my goal was set too high and I failed to achieve it, I also failed to recognise how successful my strategy could have been if moderated and made realistic. If I had said 'My goal is to be a painter,' then I might have achieved that and not been knocked off my perch by the first distraction that came.

So don't do what I did. Make sure your goal is realistic and set yourself up to succeed.

STOP WISHING

How many times have you wished for something in your life and then done nothing about it? Maybe you wished you were thinner, or fitter, or richer. If you really want something, then the first thing you have to do is to stop wishing yourself into a better life. Instead, draw up a plan and be prepared to put some effort into making your dreams come true. Remember the 3 per cent rule and take small steps.

I know it's not easy. At the moment I'm on a diet to lose weight. The surplus weight is slowly dropping off as I give up those little biscuits. The early-morning walks are beginning, and so is the careful avoidance of fat-laden foods. The plan is to achieve the goal by small steps. And the steps are well underway. But I have to work at it. I know that just wishing I was thinner isn't going to get me there.

Having a plan and implementing it is the only way to reach your goal. I am in continuous discussion with a homeless man I know who tells me he wants to have a place in the country with a shed at the bottom of the garden where he can paint pictures and then sell them in the local market.

He has his dream. What he doesn't have is a plan. I suggested that the first step to achieving his goal would be to start saving money by giving up smoking. Not only would he be helping his savings but he'd be improving his health at the same time – and what's the point in having a shed at the bottom of the garden if you're not fit enough to walk there. I even offered to send my friend on a course to help him to give up smoking. But it seems he doesn't want his goal enough. He says he can't give up smoking because it is the only thing he has. And so he will end up with the cigarettes, not the house and the garden and the shed.

If you want to achieve your goal, you will have to work out your plan and then be prepared to put some effort into the steps needed to achieve it. Plan and remember the 3 per cent rule: plan for small steps, which may be hard but not too hard, and then you will achieve your goal. You won't achieve your goal by simply wishing for it. Don't just daydream your way to your pension but be practical. To get your goal, stop daydreaming and start planning.

FIND THE RIGHT GOAL

A goal must be specific and it must be about you. There's not much point in deciding to set yourself the goal of winning the Booker Prize if you don't enjoy writing, or of wanting to own the hairdresser's on the corner if you've never cut hair. Equally, the plan you make to reach your goal must be realistic and based on your life experience. For example, if Gordon Roddick had said he would give me the money to open a chain of sandwich bars to employ homeless people it would have been useless because I don't know a thing about catering. But because he asked me to start a street paper – and I already had experience of being a printer – he was appealing to my life skills. He wasn't asking me to do something that I knew nothing about.

PAY ATTENTION TO THE DETAILS OF YOUR PLAN

Once, while working in California, I met a woman who had made helping homeless people and dealing with social justice her goal in life. She was obsessed with it to the exclusion of everything else. But her problem was that she was so focused on the big picture that she didn't pay any attention to the little details that were necessary to achieve that goal.

One thing this woman needed more than anything was a car to get around LA. You couldn't rely on public transport because you'd spend the whole day on the bus to get where you wanted and then as soon as you arrived it would be time for you to set off home again. One day she came rushing in to see me, outraged by the fascist regime of the State of California, which had repossessed her car. She needed to get her hands on a few hundred dollars soon or else it was going to be sold for a song to someone else.

It turned out that she had accumulated 10 parking fines, and in LA if you don't pay your parking fines then the police take your car.

To her it was a spiteful act. But to me it was simple. If she had made a plan and paid attention to the small details, she wouldn't have got into trouble, and her big goal of helping the homeless would have been made much easier.

Remember that the small details of your plan need as much thought, time and attention as the big goals.

MOVING THE GOAL POSTS

On the 10th anniversary of *The Big Issue,* in a very early-morning interview, a radio reporter put me on the spot. 'Well, Mr Bird,' she said, 'you have had 10 years of *The Big Issue*; what are you going to do for the next 10 years?'

I had been asked questions like this before. But this time it woke me up, probably because it was 10 years to the day that *The Big Issue* had been created.

Bobbing along for most of my life, I realised I had invented a business that bobbed along. People loved it. *The Big Issue* was a great success. It was praised from first thing in the morning to last thing at night. But our goal of helping the homeless to help themselves by supplying them with a newspaper to sell had been achieved years ago. It was time for a new goal, to move the goal posts, if we were going to progress any further. I realised that doing nothing after you have achieved your objective can sometimes even mean you slip backwards. Enjoy your success, but don't rest on your laurels for too long or you will find yourself drifting as I did.

Without hesitation I found myself replying to the interviewer: 'I have spent 10 years mending broken clocks. Now I want to spend 10 years making sure the clocks don't break in the first place.' There and then I had found a new goal. Rather than just helping people *after* they had become homeless, I was also going to try to stop people becoming homeless in the first place.

Since that interview took place, we have modified that goal to make it more realistic and practical. To aim to end homelessness in this country would be too ambitious. Instead we decided to help dismantle the causes of homelessness, and have worked out a plan of careful steps to achieve this aim.

So don't be too rigid about your goal and your plans. If you can see that your initial goal is unrealistic, then move the goal posts and increase your chances of success.

We came to see that to achieve our goal we would need to prevent homelessness from happening as well as prevent it from continuing. We have not achieved our goal, but we have worked out a plan to get to that goal. We have worked out a programme so that governments and voluntary organisations have something to go on.

Our goal seems more achievable because we have done the work on the plan. We know the steps to realise our goal. It is not a woolly, fluffy affair. It is based on the practical removal of the causes of homelessness.

PLANNING YOUR LIFE

Use goals and effective plans to help you achieve things in every area of your life. Goals are just as important in your personal life as they are in your business life. As a family man, my future is more planned than it's ever been, maybe because I have less of it than I had before.

When you realise that you won't live for ever you do need to set your goals more thoughtfully for you and for your family. Ask yourself what you want to see in 10 years' time. My goals are no different from most people with young children, I suspect: financial stability; educating and providing for the development of my children in a safe and happy environment; staying in good health so that I am around to see them grow up. Ask yourself if what you are doing now is part of the plan to achieve your goal, or simply an interesting but unnecessary distraction.

One of the strongest women I have ever had the luck to meet told me how her husband would beat her and the children on a regular basis. She said she could not see a way out of it. She had no plan and thought the abuse would go on for ever.

Then one day she got the strength together to do some planning. Every plan she came up with seemed sense-less, idealistic and impractical. So she decided to do a simple thing: she went to an advice centre. There she found out about how she could take herself and her children to a place of safety. About how she could involve the courts. And about how she could get the man excluded from her life.

It is an obvious course of action to many people. But it was not obvious to her because she had been beaten into such a situation that she could only see defeat. She couldn't imagine that an exit was possible.

This woman now helps other oppressed women out of abuse. And she knows that only by having a plan can you stop people feeling powerless and out of control. Very few plans involve great complexity, just careful staging and attention to detail, followed by action.

FOCUS

It's important not to have too many goals at any one time, as you will find it difficult to focus on all of them properly. Try to concentrate on one or two goals, and when you achieve them move onto the next. My wife is a great support and gives me a lot of encouragement. But she hates seeing me involved in so many different things that don't seem to relate to each other. She says my life is like a Christmas tree, full of very nice little lights that don't connect. So now I try to be more like a lighthouse with a big goal that shines brightly and can be seen for miles.

- Believe in your goal. Make sure it is something that excites and drives you. Don't make it so far off and distant that you lose enthusiasm about achieving it.

- Plan the stages to this goal, so that you can measure how close you are to reaching your goal and see how far you have come. Each stage should make you feel better about the attainment.

- Be clear and focused.

- Use the 3 per cent rule.

- Share your goal. Don't keep it a secret, unless you really have to. Get others to share your enthusiasm, joy and ambition. It really does help you to feel that you are going in the right direction and makes it more likely you will succeed.

- Check your plan all the time, and be prepared to modify or change it if it no longer helps your goal.

- Allow your plans some flexibility. They should be a bit like a garden with a wild meadow at the end so that the butterflies can flourish.

chapter six
CARPE DIEM

Carpe diem – or 'seize the day' as it is translated – is a great piece of advice, and if I hadn't been prepared to follow it I wouldn't have enjoyed the success I have had in my life. This is why I'm passing it on to you.

Some people think 'seize the day' means to enjoy the moment without worrying about tomorrow, but I interpret it to mean that you need to grab the opportunities that come your way. Don't let things pass you by because you're not quite ready for them. And don't put things off. Sometimes you won't get a second chance, so make sure that you're ready. You never know, such opportunities could change your life.

HOW CARPE DIEM CAN CHANGE YOUR LIFE

There have been several times in my life when I have seized an opportunity that has changed my life. The first was when I started going to evening classes at Chelsea School of Art. I had been drawing when I was in the young offenders' institution and had decided that art was the most important thing in my life. The evening classes were open to all students of the school, but I wasn't a student. I just walked in from the street and started drawing. No one seemed to notice until one evening when I was working on the biggest nude I had ever attempted. The tutor came up behind me and studied my drawing very carefully. Eventually he said, 'It is very good. I like much of your work. You seem to be always looking. What year are you in?'

I was afraid that he would throw me out when he heard that I wasn't enrolled at the college. Instead he said, 'But you must become a student. You are better than most I have seen. You must come.'

I could think of many reasons not to become a student: I had just got out from nick; I was uneducated, with no school certificate or qualifications; I wasn't a part of the world of drawers and painters; I was working at the Royal Borough of Kensington and Chelsea gardening department; I was not cut from the same cloth as the people who went to art school; I was working class; art was for others.

On the other hand, the idea of being an art student and painting all day suited me. It wasn't going to be hard to convince myself that I should go, but I knew it would be harder to convince my parents, who would have to give their permission and fill in forms. We were not a family of form-fillers.

The next day I found out that interviews for admission the following year were happening at the end of the week and that I could have one. I decided not to say anything to my parents until after I had had the interview. If I got in, then fine; if not, there was no point in having a fight about it.

I was the last person to be interviewed on the Friday afternoon. Everyone else had neat, clean black folders; I had made my own folder out of board, and it was bulky, stashed full of stuff.

At last a man came out and took my large folder from me into the interview room. But still I had to wait outside restlessly for another half-hour, pacing the floor, while they put all my pictures on the wall. When eventually I was called in I could not believe that the work was mine. The walls were completely covered; there was no space for anything else. The following week I got a letter from the art school to say that I had been accepted. I was stunned. It was a big leap to make, but I had grabbed the opportunity that had come my way, seized the day, and been successful.

However, I still had obstacles to overcome. I had to get my parents to agree, and I knew that this would be the most difficult thing to achieve. My mother was the most vocal. 'You're working class. Working-class people don't go to college,' she said. My father said he wouldn't agree and that I should get a job on a building site – it was good enough for him and it should be good enough for me.

Very rarely does an opportunity come along that doesn't require some effort on your part before it is realised. Don't expect a big break to fall into your lap. But when one does come your way, don't let difficult hurdles put you off, or you may live to regret not having taken the chance. I grabbed the opportunity to go to art school even though I had to fight to get there, because if I'd lost that moment, when I had the energy, drive and focus, I might never have got that chance again.

It took a few days but my mother and father were eventually worn down, and I got their permission to go to art school. And despite their initial distrust, they actually became proud of me. The lame duck of the family, the trouble-maker, had got himself sorted.

HOW WILL I KNOW WHEN TO SEIZE THE DAY?

Opportunities come in all sorts of shapes and sizes. Some will be obvious – you will know immediately that it is meant for you and that you should seize it. At other times, though, chances arise which are not what you thought you were looking for, or perhaps they are but they seem to come at the wrong time because you don't feel ready for them. This is what happened when Gordon Roddick asked me to start a street paper for homeless people. At first I didn't view it as a great opportunity – in fact, I was not pleased to be asked. I had recently set up a publishing company – not very successfully – and what I really wanted was some more of his money to continue doing that. I didn't want to get involved with any homeless charity. God, I had *been* flaming homeless on and off through the early decades of my life. Why would I want to re-visit disaster and failure? I thought I needed a nice, neat literary publishing business where I could hide myself from all the damage I'd accumulated from the moment I was born.

But Gordon sat there telling me what a good job I'd do, about the importance of giving homeless people a hand up and not a handout, insisting I was the right person for the job and saying he'd pay me to do a feasibility study. And of course, even though I was reluctant at first, he managed to persuade me that this was a chance I had to take.

Seizing the day – taking the plunge – involves being open to new ideas and new opportunities. Try to look at opportunity or chance from every angle. I nearly lost my chance to seize the day because I was not capable of looking 'around' the opportunity on offer. I got it in the end, but I nearly lost it because I had been too closed.

WHAT SHOULD I DO NEXT?

Once I had decided to grasp the opportunity of setting up *The Big Issue* I wanted to strike while the iron was hot. I didn't want to wait around. I knew that I could break everything down into small manageable parts. I could use my planning skills to take the fear out of such a big task. I was determined to act quickly, decisively, but without panic, and to launch *The Big Issue* within three months of receiving the finance. Most people said I was mad and that it would take us between six months to a year.

The odds did seem to be stacked against us. First of all, the homeless people we talked to were abusive and dismissive. So far as they were concerned we were just another bunch of do-gooders out to do well for ourselves but no one else. They would not be behind us at the launch.

Then there was the problem of how to start a street paper when no one else had ever done it. Or rather, that the only one already up and running was not doing well because it was just about homelessness, which limited its market.

In addition, we didn't have a proper editorial team, or any administration experience.

Why rush at something with a lack of skill and knowledge? My arguments were simple: someone might start a street paper ahead of us; many newspapers were turning against the homeless, accusing them of aggressive begging, and the longer we left it, the more difficult it would be to turn the bad press around; and I was up for it. I had the energy and the money, and anything else I lacked I would learn on the job. I was prepared to forego nights and days, and do everything necessary to get it out. The fine tweaking could happen after the launch.

There are times when long, careful planning is required. Some things you have to nurture. But there are other times when you have to throw everything into the pot and turn up the heat. You cannot afford to wait for the ideal moment. This was one of those times. I began to realise that in many ways my life had been one long preparation for this moment. All the strands of my life had come together in taking on *The Big Issue*. All the mistakes, the failures, the bruising and beatings, the begging, first for my mother's cigarettes and then eventually for my own, meant something now. All the long nights I had worked as a printer and the skills I had learned meant I was not frightened of starting a street paper. I had designed letterheads, brochures and magazines for my customers as well as for myself. I had laid out and printed books and magazines, and sold them to galleries and bookshops all over Britain. I had exported my magazines to other countries. I knew how to draw up budgets and talk the language of business. I had learned my lessons well from running a small business that had to find money to survive. And most of all I knew the homeless, the beggars, the fallen. I had lived among them and worked among them. So why hang around for months, sharpening pencils, making notes, having consultations about what to do? I had to get on with it. It had to be sooner rather than later.

I was also lucky that I had Phil to help me launch *The Big Issue*. I had met Phil a few years before through a mutual friend, and it was obvious that he was a 'get up and go' sort of man. A writer and guitarist-performer in his late twenties, he was incredibly good at talking to people, and I knew he could help me convince people that it would all work. He had a kind of professional assurance, something which I felt I lacked, a great sense of humour, and also believed in striking while the iron was hot. He kept me happy and reassured me when I got cold feet.

The launch was chaotic. Because of the association with The Body Shop, we got good press. Anita Roddick did most of the TV stuff while I did some radio work, which I realised I was good at. But it wasn't all plain sailing. Only a handful of vendors turned up on the day, including a few big mouths who just wanted to tell the press how little we knew about homelessness. On the second day the two delivery vans broke down – though as we didn't have many vendors that wasn't too much of a problem. But even if it did look a shambles, once it was launched all my fears about creating something completely new evaporated. I knew that I had done the right thing. This confidence made it easier to put up with the long hours, the insults from the homeless, and the suspicions of those working in the homeless sector, who were convinced that I was something of a second-hand car dealer. It made it easier to endure the wait for the word to get round among the homeless that you could in fact make decent money from selling the paper – and that you could also get a sense of pride because the public would talk to you, would communicate. It made it easier to deal with all the problems, from envelopes to vans to people's initial doubts. I knew that I was right to get the show on the road, and then to fix things and make changes as we went along. And I knew that the timing was right, that the day had to be seized. We were quick enough and bold enough.

Looking back, the launch of *The Big Issue* seemed to have its own momentum. It caught something about the time. Now the paper is published on every continent of the world and has inspired an international movement. It has become the biggest direct work programme for hundred of thousands of homeless people throughout the world. And it goes from strength to strength. It has started its own investment programme and has carefully looked at new ways of doing its business, which is helping the homeless to help themselves. If I hadn't seized the day none of this would have happened.

So how do you seize the day? How do you know whether to seize the moment or not? How do you know whether to grab at an opportunity? It isn't always easy to know whether you should go for something, but here are some tips to think about:

- Don't wait for the perfect moment. There is really no such thing as the ideal time when everything is perfect, so just get on and do it. Having said that, take time to listen to others who have faith in you and believe in your project. They may be able to see things that you can't.

- Be prepared to take a risk (without being reckless). All decisions involve an element of risk, whether it's starting up your own business, applying for a new job, or even entering into a new relationship. It may be safer to do nothing, but nothing is all you'll get. Do what preparation you can to increase your chances of success and to minimise the risk.

- Be prepared so that you are ready to seize the moment when it comes. I don't mean all the little details, but the big ones. Ask yourself if you have prepared enough to grab the opportunity. Make sure you know what you are talking about. Be up to speed. Do your homework. If you grasp the right opportunity having made the right preparation then you are more likely to succeed.

chapter seven
DON'T BE AFRAID OF MAKING MISTAKES

We all make mistakes. It's a fact of life, because no one is perfect and life isn't perfect. The problem is that although people pay lip service to the idea that mistakes are important, most don't really believe it. It's OK to have made a mistake in the past – so long as it's well in the past – but no one wants to admit to making a mistake now.

Two things happen if you become too afraid of making a mistake. The first is that you might be prevented from accepting new challenges which have the potential to change and improve your life. The second is that you might try to cover up your mistake – just look at how often politicians and people in public life do this, and the cover-up is usually a bigger issue than the original error. Mistakes need to be aired, and then put down as a lesson to be learned from. But you have to be able to admit to your mistakes to learn from them. Equally, unless you learn from your mistakes, you will keep on making them. So if you want to change your life, use your mistakes to gain understanding of yourself and the world around you, and see them as another step on the road to success.

THE IMPORTANCE OF MISTAKES

It has become fashionable now to talk about how important it is to make mistakes. And it's true, it is important. I've made enough mistakes in my own life to know that mistakes are how we learn, how we develop and grow. You could say I've been made by my mistakes. I do truly believe that without all the cock-ups in my life I wouldn't be writing this book.

I remember one of the first times I started talking about the importance of mistakes. When I was first starting up *The Big Issue*, I was sitting at a large meeting full of people working to help the homeless. They were very wary of me. I was not a part of the homeless world of helpers, had not come up through their ranks. Not only that, I was proposing to do something very radical: to give homeless people the means of making their own money. Not social security money, begging money or stolen money, but money they had earned.

One of the men at the meeting spoke for all of them when he explained their view that homeless people were vulnerable, needy and weak-minded people who abused themselves and acted irresponsibly. Therefore I was wrong to be doing *The Big Issue* because homeless people couldn't be trusted. It was much better if the people working to help the homeless continued to shoulder the responsibility because they were the right people to take decisions and wouldn't make any mistakes. You didn't want homeless people making mistakes.

As he talked I was reminded of those people who used to say you couldn't trust the working classes or women with the vote because they might vote 'wrong'. It was the same thing here, and it wound me up as tight as a spring. 'The problem with you,' I said, 'is that you are afraid of the homeless making their own mistakes. You don't want the homeless to make decisions because you don't trust them to get it right. And because you don't trust them they will never grow up, will never learn to get on top of their lives. If they were only capable of making dangerous decisions they would be in a mental institution, but as they are not, and are living in hostels and on the streets, we have to help them grow up. We have to give them responsibility, otherwise they will always be dependent on society. They need the freedom to make mistakes in order to grow up and learn to live better lives.'

It was the first big talk I had given, and I believed more than ever that what I was saying was right. Maybe the homeless wouldn't learn from their mistakes, and if they didn't they would pay the price just like everyone else. But they had to be given the opportunity to learn from their own mistakes or they would never change their lives.

I didn't convince the people at that meeting. I had been too blunt, trodden on too many toes and made myself even more unpopular by criticising them. But later I was proved right.

The success of *The Big Issue* showed that handouts were keeping homeless people homeless. Giving people the opportunity to make their own mistakes so they can learn and develop from them is as important for the homeless as it is for you.

The next time you wonder whether to do something new or different, don't turn the opportunity down because you're afraid of making a mistake. Mistakes happen. So what? The world isn't going to end. Get on with life, and make the most of it. Believe that your mistakes can be as important as your successes in changing your life for the better.

LEARN ABOUT YOURSELF FROM MISTAKES

Mistakes are only important if you can learn from them. One of the biggest, most humiliating mistakes of my adult life happened when I agreed to train people for the civil service. I was recruited by a guy called Tony, a private contractor with more work than he could manage, who was always on the look-out for loud, amiable, bright people to help him run courses. So when he met me at a restaurant through mutual friends he asked me if I'd like to be involved.

Saying yes was a big mistake. I knew deep down that I wasn't really suited to it. There were great holes in my learning ability, due to my sporadic childhood education. I was well aware, for example, that I was no good at learning by rote, yet I was accepting a job that involved lots of paperwork and stuff that had to be read through and learned by heart.

I still look back on those days with a kind of shiver. The money was good (which was what tempted me to do the job) and the people I was training were mainly polite. But once they realised my incompetence they treated me as a fool.

I survived a number of courses I worked on, but not successfully. As people pointed out my stupidity, my confidence vanished and I became even more of a fool. It got so bad that I couldn't even carry a tray across a canteen without dropping it. And then the big test came: a two-week course at a hotel in the country working with our leader, Tony. I will never return to Lewes in Sussex without feeling a complete fraud. Tony had chosen me in the first instance because I was loud and friendly and he believed that I was bright enough to learn quickly. I was not. I became learning-blind. I just could not answer the questions directed at me; I could not even string a sentence together. Humiliation after humiliation was piled upon me. I was the wrong person doing the wrong job, no use to man or beast.

At the end of the course even Tony had to draw a deep breath when talking about my performance. Unfortunately, the students also had to fill in a tutor assessment form. And needless to say I was coming out with minuses, with some people kind enough to give me a few ones and twos. Eventually I was dumped, but only after Tony had stuck his neck out for me.

Although that year was truly humiliating, I learned some very valuable lessons from my mistake: never try to do a job to which you are unsuited, or ask anyone else to do that either; you cannot be all things to all men; and you have to play to your strengths.

So how do you avoid making the same mistake as I did? How do you make sure that you find your strengths? How do you make sure that you learn about yourself from your mistakes? Be truthful to yourself. Spend a fair bit of time finding out what your strengths are.

DISCOVER YOUR STRENGTHS

To find out what your strengths are, listen to other people. Don't make the mistake of believing your own propaganda. My daughter once pointed out how the friendly things I said to people really made them feel a part of the company she runs. I was astonished. I always thought that small talk was one of my worst skills. But people often don't really know what they are good at. They have never done an audit of their strengths and weaknesses.

I can't count the number of times I've met people who have said things such as, 'Oh, I'm really good with people', or 'I always keep my head when the shit hits the fan', and I know it is untrue. I was thinking this yesterday as I stood in a café waiting for a sausage roll. The place was full of staff. The woman whose job it was to make the sausage roll was also telling other people what to do: keep the floor clean, put out the signs in front of the café, clear the tables, etc. And her manner, her face – even the colour of her face – told you that she was unsuited to working in a kitchen café. She was permanently angry. Having waited fifteen minutes for my sausage roll I asked what was happening to the order. Her face went a deeper red, she mumbled something; for a moment, I was the cause of all her problems. I felt sorry for the poor woman. She was in completely the wrong job. But the problem was that she clearly didn't realise this, and until she did she was never going to learn from her mistake.

You have to check that your own perception is matched by reality. In my case I can say I am good at, and have a knowledge of, printing, design and writing. I have a loud mouth, and when I talk people can hear me. So starting up a street paper and making people listen to what I have to say about homelessness was the right job for me. On the minus side, I am not good at reading a load of technical journals and paperwork, or passing exams or talking about things in which I have no interest, so a job in the civil service was totally wrong for me.

DON'T REPEAT YOUR MISTAKES

Are you one of the many people – probably with a good job, a stable life and comfortable home – who make the same mistake again and again? It might be that you keep on buying the same unflattering clothes, or choosing the same kind of untrustworthy partner, or even going on the same type of disappointing holiday. It's amazing how many times you can repeat your mistake without doing anything about it. I have a friend who always chases the same kind of men. Not long after she has caught them, they let her down. She feels bad about it but never seems to do anything to change it. You'll never get anywhere without mistakes. But you'll never get anywhere without learning from your mistakes. So look at your mistakes carefully, learn the lessons, however hard, and then remember them so you don't repeat them.

CATCH MISTAKES IN TIME

Although I believe that you can always learn something useful from your mistakes, I am not saying that you should try to cultivate them. Sometimes mistakes can be fatal or very damaging, and of course we do our best not to make them in the first place. But if you do make a mistake, then admit it quickly and try to catch it while it's still small. The longer you leave a mistake, the bigger it becomes and the worse it gets. Often a tooth only needs extraction because you didn't sort it out when it was beginning to decay.

I very nearly made a fatal mistake with *The Big Issue*. I believed my own propaganda. I believed that I was as big and as strong as everyone said I was. So I didn't notice that our market was shrinking and our sales were dropping, especially after the 9/11 attack on the Twin Towers in New York. People didn't want to linger in the streets, or if they did, they were not buying from our vendors. Sales of advertising dropped because confidence in business was hit. This had a big effect on our turnover.

I was so caught up with international developments of *The Big Issue* that I took my eye off the rabbit. And this mistake, left so long, suddenly looked terminal. Bankruptcy loomed. The brick wall was approaching very fast. We had been running for just over 10 years, but we wouldn't be around for another 10 months unless we did something fast.

We had to cut the budget and down-size. If we didn't have the money to run a big operation then we had to make it small. And we had to do it quick. So the cuts were made, and we took the hit. The company went from being the biggest and strongest social business in Britain to something much smaller – it was the only way to survive.

It was tough being the leader who had lost the lead. I felt humiliated in front of the many people – even those I thought were friends – who gloated that I was an idiot and a bad manager. And the press had a field day.

Luckily, the mistakes weren't terminal, I was given a second chance and *The Big Issue* didn't fold. We are now back at the top, flourishing and developing new social businesses. But the mistakes were not buried; they have been looked at carefully so we can see how to do things differently and better. We have learned about the importance of getting the right people, sticking like glue to your budget, keeping costs down, and informing everyone about what is happening – in effect, we've learned about good housekeeping.

But the biggest lesson I have learned and taken to heart is that if I had looked at the mistakes early on, and valued them for the knowledge they held then, we wouldn't have nearly died as a business. Even today I still hear people talk about how I destroyed *The Big Issue*, despite the fact that I have overseen its reconstruction. My mistake cost us dearly, and we are still paying the price because it lost us some of our best supporters, who may never come back to the fold.

So catch your mistakes while they are still small, and not when they have been allowed to grow out of proportion. The old saying 'A stitch in time saves nine' is both sensible and wise. Try not to set yourself up to fail and limit your mistakes. Learn what you can from small mistakes so that you don't have to make the big ones.

MISTAKES IN THE WORKPLACE

It would be much easier to catch mistakes while they are still small if we made it easier to admit to mistakes and stopped making people feel bad because they have cocked up. This is a particularly big problem in the workplace. All too often you're not allowed to put your mistakes behind you and are marked for life. But this attitude is self-defeating. Businesses need to understand how valuable mistakes can be. The companies I know that rise above the rest are the ones that seriously discuss what mistakes have meant, and learn from them. We have to change the culture that makes it so difficult to own up, so the errors can be caught earlier and the damage limited.

Obviously, there are mistakes and mistakes, and some mistakes are harder to forgive than others – for example, if politicians buy and sell influence, or line their own pockets whilst in public office. These are not mistakes that we should countenance. But most of the time, trivial political mistakes are covered up and then become worse. What a stupid waste of time.

As Tony, my teacher at the civil service college, said, 'Mistakes are always best viewed from the past.' In other words it's fine to reminisce about all the mistakes you made as a child or in your youth. Well, it's time we all admitted that we make mistakes in the present. So here's my admission:

A few weeks ago I did a talk at a college about leadership. They sent me down loads of stupid paperwork. I couldn't understand it. It was all jargon but I made the mistake of doing the talk they wanted. What I should have said was, 'Look here, if you want that jargon stuff go to someone else.' But I didn't. I went with it. Now I have the same bad taste in my mouth that I had years ago.

It shows that even an old dog like me can still make the same mistakes. There, I said it. So, relax, and don't be afraid of making mistakes. You won't get hit by thunder and lightning if you admit to making them. Just remember to expect more from yourself next time.

- Mistakes can make you stronger and more successful if you learn from them.

- Don't dwell on your mistakes, or those of others, except to learn from them. Once you have made a mistake, however bad, then understand and accept it, put it behind you, and move on.

- If you have made a mistake, be cool-headed about it and analyse it. Be objective, as if you were looking at the behaviour of another person. See what you can learn from it.

- Accept that you can't be great at everything, and don't pretend to be something you're not. Don't beat yourself up because there are some areas you're not good at – we all have weaknesses. Just concentrate on building up your strengths.

- If you have made the mistake of being in the wrong job, as I did, don't hang around. The longer you stay trying to do what you're not good at, the more confidence you will lose and the harder it will be to get the right job.

- Don't wallow in your mistakes for too long. Get on with life and make of yourself what you can.

chapter eight
STOP THINKING LIKE A VICTIM

The world is full of victims. I don't mean the millions of people who have suffered through war and conflict and injustice, but the people who spend their time feeling that life is unfair, that the world has got it in for them, and that their problems are all someone else's fault. And though you might think that people like this are bound to be from the most disadvantaged backgrounds in our society, you'd be wrong. These people are not necessarily the ones at the bottom of the social pile, stuck in prison or poverty or homelessness. In fact, many of the people who believe they are victims come from successful, comfortable backgrounds but are incapable of seeing how fortunate they are. They're not victims in any real sense of the word, but they think like a victim. Maybe you do, too. Do you ever:

- feel as though the cards are always stacked against you?

- believe it is other people who get the breaks?

- blame others for your problems?

- tell people how hard things are for you and secretly enjoy their sympathy?

If you can identify with any of those feelings, then you are someone who has become caught in the trap of thinking like a victim. And if you want to do something to change your life you have to stop it, because thinking like a victim is really nothing more than a reason not to do anything yourself. You have to stop thinking that everything that happens in your life is the fault of someone or something else, that you have no control over it, and you can't do anything about it.

ACCEPTANCE

Of course, the first step towards changing things is to accept that you are thinking like a victim. Many people find this hard. Recently I went out for dinner with someone I'd met through work and have known for a few years. In the car on the way to the restaurant, he started to tell me his woes, which centred around some bad investments he had made based on bad advice (so not his fault). But as I thought about it I realised that he was someone who always had a cloud of under-achievement hanging over him. He always complained that the cards were stacked against him – which is why he was just a millionaire instead of a multi-millionaire – that wherever he worked people didn't like him. Even now that he was working for himself, there was still something preventing him from reaching the heights of his ambition.

I realised that, despite his success, he was a classic example of someone who thought like a victim. He sounded like Bill, who has been begging for years and who I meet every now and then in the West End of London. Every time I meet Bill he is more and more angry with life. He looks thinner and his complexion is worse. Begging has not done anything for him – all the money he gets goes on his habit. But apart from the accent and a slightly more polite way of expressing anger, my friend in the car was complaining and blaming in exactly the same way as Bill. The only thing that seemed to divide them was that one had plenty and the other had nothing.

I think my friend was enjoying bending my ear about his problems, so he drove slowly and it took us ages to get to the restaurant where we were meeting his wife and some of their friends. Throughout the evening he hardly talked to anyone but just looked troubled. So I have to say that at the end of the meal I tried to find another way of getting home, because people who think like victims are, in fact, very boring. They are so obsessed with themselves and their own misery that they seldom have time to think of other people. But there was no escape; I had to go with him. And, as predicted, he started to talk to me again about his difficult past and all the obstacles that had been placed in his way by other people. I wanted to get to a point in the journey where I could give him some advice. For years I had tried to avoid telling him what I thought, which was, 'Hey, you're just another victim. The difference between you and the victims I know is that you have a private hedge around your problem. You have a car, a timeshare in the Canaries, savings. But really you're just like the rest of the people I know who hide behind the excuse that life has dealt you a dirty hand of cards.'

I wanted to say all this, but he never seemed to give me the chance. Eventually when we got out of the car and stood on the lawn in front of his expensive house, better than any house I have ever had, I managed it. 'You are going to have to give up being a victim,' I said. 'You have been a victim all your life. As you have climbed the ladder of success you have ignored all the evidence that you are not a victim. Instead you have spent your life feeling sorry for yourself.' I didn't want to have that kind of chat with my friend right outside his house. But I couldn't watch him devalue the life, the family and the prosperity that he had.

He screwed up his face. 'Is that what you think? You must be mad! Thinking me a victim? Me, of all people?' I stuck to my guns and replied, 'Yes, you a victim. The cards always stacked against you. Life dealing you a number of bad blows. Nobody seeing your true potential. You don't sound any different from the homeless people I work with. The same problem: always looking for some reason to explain why you have not got what you want.' But he wasn't listening and just went into the house.

I stood for a few minutes and walked down the street. Why did nobody understand me? Why was I always being misunderstood? Why was it that life had . . .

I'm joking! But seriously, until my friend recognised the truth of what I was saying, he wasn't going to improve his life.

NO EXCUSES

It's always refreshing when you meet people who you expect will complain about their lot in life – possibly because they have some reason to complain – and they don't. I quite regularly go to prisons to give talks to the prisoners about how I got out of crime and changed my life. It was on one such visit to Wandsworth Prison, during a chat with prisoners after my talk, that I realised none of them were complaining about being hard done by, or blaming somebody else for their crimes, or using a hard-luck story as an excuse.

Because that's what being a victim is really all about. It's about giving yourself a brilliant excuse for bad behaviour, for not doing well enough in life. You may well have had a hard life or a difficult time, but so have lots of people because life isn't fair. Why should you expect everything in life to go without a hitch? The important thing is what you decide to do about it. Are you going to spend the rest of your life wallowing in self-pity and making yourself more miserable, or are you going to do what you can to make the best of things?

Up until a few years before I started *The Big Issue* I always had this reserve tank of self-pity. While having a drink I could change from conviviality to aggression to self-pity. My trick was to blame my anti-social behaviour on being screwed up in my early years. It took a while but in the end I could see that to continue to behave aggressively and cover it with lashings of self-pity was no longer an acceptable excuse.

DO SOMETHING ABOUT IT

I have met many homeless people who have made me realise how self-defeating it is to think like a victim. They cling to their role as victim like a life-line, and would be lost without their self-pity. So, as I started *The Big Issue*, though I would still drink to excess, I stopped using the same old excuses. I couldn't keep going on about how life had been so hard for me, that I was only just managing. I stopped thinking like a victim because I met so many people who did the same that my own victim claims started to look puny and self-indulgent.

One of the first people to show me how destructive it is to think like a victim was a very bright woman. She was in her mid-forties, had been a squatter and then an unsuccessful beggar. *The Big Issue* came just in time for her. She sold enough papers to have some kind of life.

We helped her get indoors and then, as she had teaching skills, we helped her to teach literacy, which she was good at. But it was never enough. There was always something that I, or one of my team, had not done for her. She grumbled there were people stopping her doing her job – the teaching authorities, headmasters, the local council – she had a long list of complaints about how other people had failed her. Instead of looking at how much was being done to help her, she just went on and on, feeling disgruntled and dissatisfied.

You can't carry on feeling sorry for yourself when you see what it does to someone like this. Such people are held back by their victimhood. So I got it out of my system because I saw other people using it destructively, to excuse themselves for not moving on to something else. I started to see how self-pity clouds the sky of opportunity and gets you nowhere. My self-pity collapsed under the weight of meeting hundreds of other people's self-pity. And my realising that it did not get them anywhere.

So if you are aware that you have started to think of yourself as one of life's victims, try looking at the lives of others. When you meet actual victims, you will often find people who refuse to be defeated, though everything seems stacked against them. You will see humanity at its best. And you will see them as an inspiration for all of those who want to blame the world and their victimhood for not getting what they want.

- Self-delusion takes many forms, but seeing yourself as the victim is one of the easiest to get rid of.

- Dump self-pity. I'm not saying that you haven't got reasons to feel sorry for yourself, but self-pity will hold you back.

- Fill your mind with positive thoughts. You only have so much mind space. Don't fill it up with all the reasons not to do something. Instead, think about how you can do something and make a plan for how you are going to get there.

- Rise above events. Be analytical if something bad happens. Instead of letting it depress you, try to review it objectively to discover why and how it happened. Don't blame a failure on other people, or see it as a conspiracy against you – there may be people who dislike you, however likeable you are, but don't use this as an excuse to stay back when you could be ascending the heights. When you have done what you can to understand the problem, take action and then move on.

- Do what you can to ensure you don't become a genuine victim. For a while it was popular to say that the way you walked and the way you held yourself made you more or less liable to personal attack and mugging. I am sure there is something in this. Don't walk, talk or think like a victim. Don't allow yourself the luxury of wallowing in your own self-pity. It won't get you anywhere. Remember that most real victims don't have the luxury of indulging in their victimship.

- Don't let misfortune or problems hold you back. Get out and prove that they can become a spur to your success.

chapter nine
KNOCK OFF KNOCKING

Knockers are people who define themselves by the failure of others. They are never a part of the problem, although everyone else is. Or, as I say when I'm being playful, 'cogitation through castigation and accusation'. In other words, knockers spend their time thinking of ways to criticise other people for letting them down. It used to be confined to comic characters on TV and film – you know, the nosy neighbours having a go at everyone else on the street. But knocking others seems to have become something of a national habit. Everybody's doing it – sniping, complaining and criticising. I've spent whole evenings with people who have done nothing but knock work colleagues, television actors, government ministers, absent friends. I have often participated, and am just as guilty of at times building myself up at the expense of everyone else's failure. And I'm not saying that we shouldn't enjoy doing it from time to time with our mates. Knocking people for not being as good as ourselves makes us feel that our own little life is not so bad, which is why we all love a good story about the failure of pop stars, campaigners, politicians and whoever else becomes public property. But if it becomes an ingrained habit, then you have a problem, because it's a well-known fact that knockers have never changed anything worth changing.

KNOCKING ACHIEVERS

Of course, it's difficult to avoid the knocker's view of life. One of the biggest 'commodities' today is knocking people who achieve, who try to do something. Castigating other people and bringing them down is what seems to sell newspapers and makes us listen to the radio and watch TV programmes. Exposing the failures of companies is big business – for example, highlighting the failure of people who think they are better than us, but who we soon find out are bent, greedy, vain, or just plain dumb.

Well, you might argue, there's a lot to complain about. We do live in a world where we are 'let down' by politicians and bosses, by banks and telephone businesses. It would seem that we do have more reason to complain. And yes, we do have to be critical. We do have to weigh up the behaviour of those around us. Bad things are still going on and I'm not saying we should just shut up about them. That would mean free rein for bad practice and corruption. But becoming an expert on the failure of others and knocking them for it doesn't bring us any nearer to solving the problem. You don't have to fill a gap in your life by moaning and whinging. If you're not careful, it will become a reason not to do anything yourself. Don't just complain. Try and change the bad things about your life, and the life of others.

QUESTION NEGATIVE VIEWS

Knockers see life through grey-tinted spectacles, viewing everything in a negative way. And if you start to see the world in this light you lose the incentive to change things for the better. If everyone is corrupt and all our institutions no good, as knockers would have us believe, then there is no point in trying to do anything all. But of course this isn't a true picture. Be careful when hearing a story that knocks someone or something not to accept the negative view without thinking about it or checking it. For example, the other day I heard a radio station lead the news with an exposé: trainee NASA astronauts had been getting drunk while in training. NASA was mortified, but I was amazed it even made the news. After all, those squeaky clean astronauts are human and capable of making mistakes, just like the rest of us. But the whole incident was described as another major institution of the world having let us down again. And I could quote a hundred thousand occasions in the year when a piece of information has been sold to you in some form or another to prove that really you can't trust anyone, and that everyone is on the fiddle. If you unreasonably expect people or institutions to be perfect, then of course you will be disappointed, but it doesn't mean that we have to be downhearted and negative.

BE CONSTRUCTIVE, NOT DESTRUCTIVE

Knockers don't actually do anything. Because knocking other people makes you feel superior, you don't need to change anything about your own life. My mother was always knocking people, because of their religion, race, class – anything and everything.

Nothing escaped her. She thought everyone was useless and 'at it', and implied that she could do everything better. But she never did. If you want to be a doer, a creator and a builder, then you must steer well away from knocking or from people who knock, and find yourself a more positive outlook.

You might think that knocking is not very pleasant but at least it's harmless. After all, knockers only talk. But in fact, I think that knocking is very harmful – for it seeks to tear down and destroy.

I caught the habit of knocking from my mum, and, as a young man, even though I was hardly leading a blameless life myself, I would always criticise other people. Then, in the late sixties, when I was 21, I got involved in one of the biggest bunch of knockers around: a revolutionary party. They turned knocking into a form of religion. Most of their energy was spent getting people dissatisfied with Capitalism to unite and fight against the ruling class in order to make a better system. My hatred of all those people who ran the system so badly, now found a faith, a belief to follow. But the trouble was that they didn't know how to create a better system, so instead they made knocking and destroying an end in itself.

During the first year of my involvement with the revolutionary knockers, there was a summer camp. About five hundred of us went off to Essex and for two weeks we stayed in a farmer's field in marquees. It was fascinating. Everyone, including all other revolutionaries, had got it wrong. The Labour government of the time was rotten through and through. The business world was full of Fascists just waiting to destroy our freedom. The working classes were being treated appallingly, with their basic rights and living conditions falling by the day. And so it went on. Five hundred of us spent all of our time developing a knocking philosophy to destroy the system, instead of trying to analyse what was wrong with the system, or doing anything positive to change things for the better.

Jump forward 40 years and what we were saying in our tents in the Essex countryside seems to be shared by more and more people, by respectable members of society who are given over to a gripe. I can't help feeling that all the whinging and knocking all grew out of those Essex fields. It may be middle-class and respectable now, but if the knocking cannot suggest constructive alternatives, then it is equally worthless.

KNOCKING AND THE HOMELESS

Sometimes I think people don't realise how dangerous their constant knocking can be and I wonder, if they did, whether they would do it so much. I often get a lot of knocking from the homeless. Most of the time I'm strong enough to take it, but just occasionally it can get to me. I remember once standing in a crowded pub trying to get to the bar. As I got nearer I saw a very large man pushing his way forward. I recognised him as a seller of *The Big Issue*. When he saw me his face turned from mildness to wildness, and he shouted across the bar to me, 'Hey, I've got a bone to pick with you.' So I shouted back, equally loudly, 'And I've got a bone to pick with you.'

I have the loudest voice of anyone I know. He heard me. So we went to stand together outside the crowded pub where he proceeded to pick his bone and launched into a long list of all that was wrong with *The Big Issue*: the staff didn't care for homeless people; the magazine didn't print enough articles about the problems they were facing; it wasn't really that useful; and a number of other complaints that had been made about *The Big Issue* from both homeless people and others.

I listened patiently for a while until suddenly I had had enough. 'Well, if it's that bad,' I said, 'and that useless, I'll go into the office tomorrow and close it down. I'll just shut it down, then you don't have to be used and exploited by it. Yes, that's what I'll do.' And I said this in the same tone of voice that he had used. *The Big Issue* vendor looked at me with his mouth open. You could see the shock as he registered that *The Big Issue*, which he had said was worth nothing and had done nothing for him, might be no more. His knocking comments got him a little more than he'd bargained for and a big dose of reality.

Eventually he said that he would like to buy me a drink and that actually *The Big Issue* had kept him out of prison and enabled him to pay for his room. So it had done him some good. He may have been knocking it but he didn't want it to close. And of course I had no intention of shutting down *The Big Issue*. But I learned that if you try to do something in life then you have to be prepared for people to criticise you. Don't give up and don't let knockers put you off. Of course you might not get everything right – no one is perfect, so you will make mistakes – but remember that the people who criticise you have done nothing themselves, and don't have the courage to try new things.

Sometimes the complaints from the homeless were so overwhelming that I did feel like closing *The Big Issue*. It was the reduction of all of our labours to nothing that annoyed me. But mostly I kept my cool because it was obvious that the homeless people were victims. That their knocking everyone else but themselves was a sign of their problem, and knocking was a part of the crisis. But it was the part that seemed to say, 'Knock rather than do. Knock rather than change.'

Homeless people have often gone through so much, and lost so much, that you can forgive them for lashing out at everyone. To some extent it is understandable. But for people who have jobs, houses and regular holidays there is no excuse for knocking instead of doing. If you feel strongly about something then don't moan, do. And if you can't do then don't moan. Moaning will take years off your creative life.

The Big Issue vendor departed years ago. I don't know if he got a job, went to prison, returned home, or died. That is the nature of *The Big Issue*. People come and work with us, and many of them disappear. I would like to think that he went somewhere better. But I am convinced that if he developed a healthy attitude towards life while at *The Big Issue* it might be because he gave up being a knocker and became a doer.

PUT YOUR ENERGY INTO SOMETHING MORE USEFUL

It's amazing how much time and energy people can spend on knocking. The other week I was travelling in a cab when, without any prompting from me, the cab driver started telling me his views on the latest performance of a major London football team. His almost forensic knowledge of the game and the club was breathtaking. He went into incredible detail about the manager, the owner and the players as he dismissed their performance. Imagine if he had put that energy and knowledge to some useful purpose. Perhaps he could have been a great TV or radio commentator, or a sports journalist. All he needed was some training. But to do that he would have had to take some of his knocking energy and use it constructively.

I understand how tempting it is to join the knocking brigade. It's a chance to air your views and even be a bit clever without actually having to do anything else. And it's a way of telling yourself you are above it all, and that you could do those things if you wanted to but you've chosen not to. We're all guilty of it, but if you do it on a regular basis then you'll eventually find it very hard to make changes in your life.

If you dump your knocking you can use the energy to change things about yourself. You might begin to relax and look around for opportunities. Remember, the person who is most hurt by knocking is often you, because you are holding yourself back by negative thinking.

- Don't give up on yourself. The thought that you might fail should not stop you making an effort. And if you do fail, at least you tried, which is better than most people.

- Do something about the changes you would like to see instead of just talking about them. If you feel that passionately about something, get your act together and do something about it. If you think the world is full of bad political leaders then become a leader yourself, even in a small way. Stop complaining about what doesn't work. Channel negative energy into doing something positive and useful that will change your life for the better. More action, less chat.

- Look at yourself before you judge others. We know that we could all do with a stiff dose of criticism, but the best way of making sure we don't get it is by knocking. The defences go up and the gate is closed, along with the ears.

- Reserve your observations for something in which you are knowledgeable. Don't dismiss someone or something you know nothing about. If you don't know the circumstances, refrain from putting in your pennyworth. And if you are ignorant or unsure and want to comment, find out more about it. Replace knocking with analysis, research, knowledge and action. Wrongly criticising someone plays into the hands of the corrupt and incompetent because you devalue worthwhile criticism.

- The more you knock the more you stay exactly where you are in your life. So give up the knocking and become the doer in your own life.

chapter ten
NO ROCKET SCIENCE, PLEASE

From the way some people talk you would think that to make even the most basic change in life requires the knowledge of a rocket scientist because everything is so complicated and difficult. But I hope this book has shown you that changing your life can be easy if you just keep it simple; if you start with the basic, small things and build up. That's how I changed my life: by doing simple things. I have never had a really clever thought in the whole of my life. I like things to be straightforward, not complex, and I don't think you need to be a rocket scientist to live a happy life.

GENIUS IS NOT REQUIRED

Most things in life can be done by most people. If you want to succeed at something, then try it and persevere – and if at first you don't succeed, then try again.

Obviously some people will find some things easier than others, but you don't have to be a genius to learn most things. Even someone as successful as the billionaire Richard Branson isn't a genius. He got to where he is today by application and perseverance. If you dismantle all the deals he has done, good and bad, you'll find that they are not particularly complex, and certainly not rocket science. They do take skill and a lot of determination. But Branson didn't use rocket science to build his empire. He just put the building blocks of business together. If you use simple steps and build on what you already know, you will find success more easily.

As I have said on countless occasions, *The Big Issue* was not an act of genius. It was an act of simple need. It worked because enough people bought the paper from the army of vendors who happened to be available to make some money.

We have to get away from the idea that change can only be the result of a long chain of events that are outside our control or our knowledge. You can start to change your life a few minutes after you have put this book down.

LEARN THE BASICS

If you want things to change in your life, you need to make sure that you have got the fundamentals right first. Look to the simple and not the complicated. A lot of people miss out on the simple lessons that need to be learned in life and so they fall flat on their face. Remember you have to learn to walk before you can run. My parents are a great example of people who didn't learn to walk before trying to run. They were very skilful people – my mother had been a bus conductor, and so her mental arithmetic was good, and my father could build houses, repair cars, even cook the finest cakes and breads you had ever tasted – but they were in permanent crisis because they didn't know how to manage the most fundamental things in their life, particularly money. They didn't face up to anything, felt constantly beaten down. Yet, if they had looked at the crisis in their lives they would have seen that most of it could be solved very simply. But because they had never learned to save money instead of spending it on things they didn't need, they were never able to sort out their lives. So get the basic, simple things in life sorted out first before you start to solve the bigger problems.

DON'T OVER-COMPLICATE

Sometimes it can be hard to think of change because there are problems in the way that seem too difficult to dismantle. But I often think we over-complicate matters, and this becomes a good excuse for not doing anything. If you dress the problems of your life up as being too deeply complicated then you are hiding from the fact that you could do something at this very moment to move your life forward. Don't talk yourself into believing that you can't change, or think that you need expert help to get things going. I remember a friend of mine who wanted to improve her fitness. She was looking forward to the arrival of her step machine, which had been recommended by experts and which she had ordered from America. While she waited, she fretted about her health, saying that she couldn't wait to get on with her new regime. I pointed out to her that she had steps in the house already and could be using them. The look on her face was extraordinary! Yes, she had overlooked the really simply solution to her problem and instead put the whole affair into orbit, to be solved by rocket scientists and their rocket science equipment.

So have a go at simple solutions. Want to be healthy? Try exercise. You don't need a PhD to set your morning alarm half an hour earlier in order to do some sit-ups, or the latest diet book from Detroit or Denver or Darlington to get rid of the flab. You just need to simply set the clock yourself. Want to stop smoking? Then try not putting a cigarette into your mouth and lighting the other end. That is the most simple solution. Yes, I know you need willpower, too, but you don't have to be super-human to develop willpower. Stop thinking of all the complicated reasons why you can't stop smoking, and just try the simple act of giving up. I did it and I'm not a genius. Just remember the 3 per cent rule – one step at a time, one day at a time – and get on with it. And if you find that you just can't put the effort in, then get your rocket scientist to put a rocket up your arse!

Remember: simple is often best. So don't make things more complicated than they need to be. The answers are often less complicated than you think. One of the best stories I ever heard about over-complicating things was when NASA spent years and millions of dollars developing a special pen that could write upside-down in space. When at last the project was finished, NASA offered the finely honed piece of engineering as a gift to the Soviet Space Programme. The Russians simply smiled and said, 'We use pencils.'

DO THE SIMPLE THINGS FIRST

Of course, life's problems are not always simple, but if you look for simple solutions first, you will find the bigger problems are easier to solve, too. For example, *The Big Issue* offers the homeless the means of making their own money legally. It doesn't offer them a cure-all. And because of that many of them complain. But I look at them after they have spent a few weeks earning their own money by selling *The Big Issue* and I can see how many of them have changed. Their priorities alter. Now they want to know where they can go from there. Doing a simple thing like giving people the chance to become self-financing is extraordinary because it often puts their problems into a different perspective. They have taken a small step towards changing their lives and suddenly the bigger steps seem more possible. Selling *The Big Issue* won't get rid of the haunting nights, the hunger and the violence, but it can help people to grow in confidence.

I have rarely found a problem so complicated that nothing can be done to solve it. However big the problem, there is usually something that can either improve the situation, or make you feel that the task is manageable. Often this is the beginning of the move. But once you have done all the simple things, you can tackle the more difficult problems. It's just like doing an exam – you answer the easy questions first so you get into the swing of things, and don't look at the hard questions until the end, by which time you are on a roll and ready to believe that anything is possible.

So if you want to change your life, tackle problems while they are still knee-high to a grasshopper. Don't leave things like filling in your application form till the last minute so that you don't have time to fill it in adequately. Prepare for everything you can well in advance so that things don't become too complicated. Then you can leave rocket science to the rocket scientists.

- Always keep it simple. Don't complicate matters by trying too many things at the same time.

- Ask yourself the right questions so that you know what needs to be changed.

- Be honest about the problems. If you are part of the problem recognise it, and start to become part of the solution.

- Change is often perceived to be beyond your reach. All it takes is the honesty and the effort to get there.

- Get the easy bits out of the way first. You'll often find they help with the more difficult bits later.

- Believe in your ability to change and in the power of small change to make big change.

- Realise your full potential by enjoying every little small step you make.

- And remember: you will soon become a good example to many others.

CONCLUSION

I wrote this book because I wanted my own experiences in life to help people help themselves. I did not want it to be full of clever business management speak, or to present a picture of some shiny, saintly life that I should have lived. I wanted it to show the contradictions of living life when you are struggling to find a way out from under the big rock that lies on top of you. And I wanted to show that this struggle to pull myself up still goes on. It is not something that is a part of my history, buried in some long-ago time.

Most of the stories I read about people who seek admiration for their lives, or their fortunes, or both, talk about mistakes or problems and difficulties they have had in the dim and distant past. And we can all admit to these, so long as they aren't too recent, and the mistakes are more comical than they are tragic, or the wrongdoings more pathetic than they are vicious.

I cannot be a part of that. As I said, I am still living with the crazy things that were done to me and that I did to myself. I still sometimes feel a loss of purpose and focus in my life. And yet I still function as a man who has a lot to contribute. I am not a failure, I am not one of the fallen.

I hope you have found the advice in this book useful. Strangely, I wish that I had been able to read it when I was growing up. And, I have to admit, it is the kind of book that I still need today. I still have to be reminded of the 3 per cent rule. I still need to remember not to fall into the victim trap. I still have to admit that it is useful to reflect on the need to think for myself.

I hope this book will act as a kind of guide for you – not a book on which to build your life, rather a book to remind you of some of the things you can sort out, and to warn you of some of the big mistakes that I have made so you can avoid making them yourself.

I have used my life in order to paint a kind of story-board. I wanted to entertain you, not bore you with clean and fine examples where everything has gone extremely well, thank you. I wanted to get you thinking and acting. And to see the need to rise above mistakes, then move on with new knowledge.

I hope this book means something to you. It certainly meant a lot to me while writing it.

ABOUT THE AUTHOR

John Bird is the co-founder and editor-in-chief of *The Big Issue*, a news and current affairs magazine launched in September 1991. It is written by professional journalists and sold on the streets by homeless vendors looking to break the cycle of poverty and homelessness. Vendors buy the magazine at a wholesale rate and sell it, keeping the profit for themselves. They are self-employed and encouraged to be responsible for handling their earnings.

John was born into a London–Irish family in a slum-ridden part of Notting Hill just after the Second World War. Homeless at five, in an orphanage at seven, he began to fail over and over again in every area of his life. From the age of 10 onwards he was shoplifting, housebreaking and stealing whatever he could lay his hands on. Vandalism and arson were also among the crimes he committed.

In his late twenties, and after several prison sentences, John became involved in politics. He also fathered three children, became a printer and successfully ran his own small business. At the age of 45, his many life experiences enabled him to start production of *The Big*

Issue. He has spent the last 17 years in charge of the development of *The Big Issue* – which is now an international movement and provides opportunities for people facing homelessness to help themselves. It forges partnerships with social entrepreneurs to launch businesses for social change in cities worldwide. Setting up street papers to help socially excluded people is central to this.

John Bird was awarded the MBE for 'services to homeless people' by Her Majesty the Queen in June 1995. He is a Fellow of John Moores University, Liverpool, a Visiting Professor at Lincoln University, and a Doctor of Letters at Oxford Brookes University. In 2003, he was chosen by the Queen as one of the Most Important Pioneers in Her Majesty's Reign. In 2004, he received from the United Nations a Scroll of Excellence for his international work in poverty, presented by the President of Kenya at the Habitat Celebration in Nairobi. In the same year he also won a public vote by BBC London as London's Living Legend.

INDEX

John Bird's Quick Reads, also available from Vermilion

❏ **How to Change Your Life in 7 Steps** 9780091907037 **£1.99**
A shorter version of *Change Your Life*, this lively self-help book outlines seven simple rules that could help you change your life. Whether you want to get a new job, quit smoking, give up drinking or go back to college, *How to Change Your Life in 7 Steps* explains how you can take what you've been given and turn it into something you'll be proud of.

❏ **The 10 Keys to Success** 9780091923600 **£1.99**
Are you struggling to achieve what you want? John Bird will show you just how simple success can be. With simple, practical advice, such as 'Stop looking for approval from others', John shows us that we can all achieve whatever we want. We just need to go after it.

FREE POSTAGE AND PACKING

Overseas customers allow £2.00 per paperback

BY PHONE: 01624 677237

BY POST: Random House Books
c/o Bookpost, PO Box 29, Douglas
Isle of Man, IM99 1BQ

BY FAX: 01624 670923

BY EMAIL: bookshop@enterprise.net

Cheques (payable to Bookpost) and credit cards accepted

Prices and availability subject to change without notice.
Allow 28 days for delivery.
When placing your order, please mention if you do not wish to receive any additional information.

www.rbooks.co.uk